More Knitting Wheel Tools

Have you discovered the easy way to knit? The knitting wheel (a.k.a. knitting loom) is your key to creating a whole new world of fashion. It's so simple, even a child can do it. And since there are no slippery needles to grip, the knitting wheel is the perfect creative tool for anyone whose fingers are sometimes stiff or painful.

In this book, you'll use the Knit, Purl, and Loop Stitches, but you'll go way beyond the basics to knit hats, mitts, slippers, socks—even a blanket or poncho. There are so many fascinating techniques and new wheel shapes to help you create these fun designs! Learn how to change colors, fringe-as-you-go, make short rows, and create I-cord. We've also included a variety of ways to cast on and instructions on how to felt your knitwear!

For more knitting loom projects, visit your retailer or go to www.leisurearts.com to find Leisure Arts leaflet #4372 *Knitting Wheel Fashions.*

- -

KNITTING WHEELS

The **round wheel**, also known as a knitting wheel, loom, spool, and reel, can be made out of nylon, wood, or plastic. Round wheels come in many sizes. We used five sizes for our projects. They have 12, 24, 31, 36 and 41 pegs. The round wheels can be used to make a tubular piece great for hats and small socks, and also a flat piece great for scarves. Some of our patterns are worked in a Raised Crossed Stitch for better elastic action, also known as Crossed Stocking Stitch.

The **straight wheel**, also known as a knitting board, straight loom, rectangle loom, and infinity rake, can be made out of nylon or wood. The straight wheel comes in different lengths ranging from $9^1/2$" to 60"/24 cm to 152.5 cm long and can be used for a variety of projects. We used a 15" (38 cm) straight wheel that has 36 pegs in 18 pairs and a side peg on each end used to anchor the yarn during work. We also used four sizes that each has a peg on each end in addition to the side pegs. They have 26, 38, 50 and 62 pegs.

Thick, flat, double-sided reversible knitting can be produced on the straight wheel – great for a warm baby blanket and scarves that won't curl. You can also make flat projects the same as you can make them on a round wheel, but since you're not as limited by the number of pegs, you can make a poncho and a sweater. The straight loom can even be used for circular knitting to make mitts, socks, and a wallet.

OTHER TOOLS

Knitting wheel tool - Some wheels come with a special tool that is used to help you lift the bottom loop on each peg over the top loop. The tool can also be purchased separately. A yarn needle, knitting needle, and even a nut pick can be used for the tool.

Crochet hook - Some of the projects require a crochet hook to work the cast on or bind off row. Use size K (6.5 mm) or any size large enough to catch strand(s) of yarn.

Yarn - Some of the projects included are made holding two strands of yarn together. This is a great way to achieve wonderful results combining some of the specialty yarns available.

LEISURE ARTS, INC.
Little Rock, Arkansas

Faux Feather Boa

◧◨▢▢ **EASY**

Finished Size: 84" (213 cm) long

MATERIALS

SUPER BULKY 6

Super Bulky Weight Yarn
[2.8 ounces, 68 yards
(80 grams, 62 meters) per skein**]**:
   2 skeins
24 Peg round wheel or larger or 36 peg straight
   wheel
Knitting wheel tool
Yarn needle

GAUGE: In pattern,
         12 stitches and 18 rows = 4" (10 cm)

BOA

Chain cast on 7 pegs in reverse order **(Fig. 8e, page 42)**.

Boa is worked as flat knitting, using the e-wrap method for all knit stitches throughout.

Row 1: Knit across.

Row 2: Make loop stitch **(Figs. 14a-e, page 46)**, (knit 1, make loop stitch) 3 times.

Repeat Rows 1 and 2 for pattern until Boa measures approximately 84" (213 cm) long, ending by working Row 1.

Work chain one bind off across all pegs **(Figs. 21a-c, page 50)**.

Weave in yarn ends.

Basket Hat

⬛⬛☐☐ **EASY**

Finished Size: Fits most adults

Sizing Note: The type of yarn that you use (whether it's soft or has more body) and the tension you have when you wrap the yarn, greatly effects your gauge and thus the finished size. Therefore, you can easily adjust the size of your hat by the yarn you choose and your tension.

MATERIALS

Bulky Weight Yarn
[3 ounces, 123 yards
(85 grams, 113 meters) per skein**]**:
    2 skeins
36 Peg round wheel
Knitting wheel tool
Yarn needle

Hat is worked as circular knitting, using two strands of yarn held together throughout.

GAUGE: In Body pattern,
        12 stitches and 24 rows = 6" (15 cm)

Use the e-wrap method for all knit stitches throughout.

ROLLED BRIM

E-wrap cast on all pegs.

Rounds 1-8: Knit around.

BODY

Rounds 1-4: (Knit 2, purl 4) around **(Figs. 13a-d, page 46)**.

Rounds 5 and 6: Knit around.

Rounds 7-10: Purl 3, knit 2, (purl 4, knit 2) around to last peg, purl 1.

Rounds 11 and 12: Knit around.

Rounds 13-30: Repeat Rounds 1-12 once, then repeat Rounds 1-6 once **more**.

Cut yarn leaving an 18" (45.5 cm) length.

Work gathered method to remove Hat from wheel and to close top of Hat **(Figs. 20a & b, page 50)**.

Weave in yarn ends.

Visor Cap

 EASY

Finished Size: Fits most adults

Sizing Note: The type of yarn that you use (whether it's soft or has more body) and the tension you have when you wrap the yarn, greatly effects your gauge and thus the finished size. Therefore, you can easily adjust the size of your cap by the yarn you choose and your tension.

MATERIALS

Medium Weight Variegated Yarn
[3 ounces, 146 yards
(85 grams, 134 meters) per skein]:
  1 skein
36 Peg round wheel
Knitting wheel tool
Yarn needle

Cap is worked using two strands of yarn held together throughout.

GAUGE: 9 stitches and 12 rows = 4¹/₄" (10.75 cm)

VISOR

Visor is worked as flat knitting, using the e-wrap method for all knit stitches throughout.

E-wrap cast on 15 pegs.

Rows 1 and 2: Knit across.

Row 3 (Decrease row): Decreasing first and last pegs *(Figs. 15a & b, page 47)*, knit across: 13 pegs used.

Rows 4-6: Repeat Rows 1-3: 11 pegs used.

Row 7 (Increase row): Knit across, e-wrap increase 1 peg *(Fig. 16, page 48)*: 12 pegs used.

Rows 8-10: Repeat Row 7, 3 times: 15 pegs used.

Rows 11 and 12: Knit across.

To form Visor, lift up bottom edge toward inside of wheel and place loops from cast on row over used pegs *(Fig. 18, page 49)*.

Row 13: Knit across, lifting the bottom 2 loops on each peg over the top loop and off the peg.

BODY

Begin circular knitting.

Round 1: Purl across *(Figs. 13a-d, page 46)*; e-wrap cast on all empty pegs: 36 pegs used.

Rounds 2 and 3: Purl around.

Knit each round until Body measures approximately 5" (12.5 cm).

Purl 3 rounds.

TOP WEDGES

Work flat knitting across 6 pegs for each Wedge, continuing to use the e-wrap method.

Row 1 (Decrease row): Decreasing last peg, knit across: 5 pegs used.

Rows 2-5: Repeat Row 1, 4 times: one peg is left in this Wedge.

Cut yarn leaving a long length for sewing and pull through remaining loop.

Work same as first Wedge, for a total of 6 Wedges, beginning each Wedge by placing a slip knot on the next peg to count as first E-wrap.

Sew sides of Wedges together.

Weave in yarn ends.

Fur Stripes Ear Flap Hat ● ● ● ● ● ● ● ●

◼◼▢▢ **EASY**

Finished Size: 14¹/₂{17-19¹/₄}"/37{43-49} cm circumference

Size Note: Instructions are written for child's size with adult sizes Small and Large in braces { }. Instructions will be easier to read if you circle all the numbers pertaining to your size. If only one number is given, it applies to all sizes.

MATERIALS

MEDIUM 4

Medium Weight Variegated Yarn
[5 ounces, 244 yards
(141 grams, 223 meters) per skein]:
1 skein

BULKY 5

Bulky Weight Long Eyelash Yarn
[1.75 ounces, 60 yards
(50 grams, 54 meters) per skein]:
1 skein
31{36-41} Peg round wheel
Knitting wheel tool
Crochet hook, size K (6.5 mm)
Yarn needle

Hat is worked using two strands of yarn held together throughout.

GAUGE: 9 stitches and 12 rows = 4¹/₄" (10.75 cm)

Use the e-wrap method for all knit stitches throughout.

CORD

Make a tassel as follows: Cut four 8" (20.5 cm) lengths of medium weight yarn. Holding all of the strands together, fold them in half forming a loop and place the loop around the first peg, with the ends to the inside of the wheel **(Fig. 1a)**. Cut a 9" (23 cm) length and wrap it tightly around the folded strands, close to peg; knot yarn to secure **(Fig. 1b)**.

Fig. 1a　　　　　**Fig. 1b**

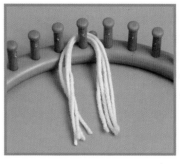 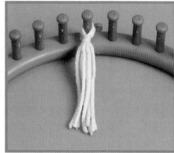

Row 1: Holding two strands of medium weight yarn together, e-wrap the first peg and bring tassel loop over wrap, chain increase 1 peg (to right of tassel) **(see Chain Increase, page 48)**.

Row 2: Knit 2, chain increase 1 peg: 3 pegs used.

Row 3: Knit 3.

Make I-cord for 5" (12.5 cm) **(Figs. 26a & b, page 54)**.

EAR FLAP

Ear Flap is worked as flat knitting.

Row 1 (Increase row)**:** Skip 1 **(see Skip A Peg, page 48)**, knit across, chain increase 1 peg: 4 pegs used.

Row 2 (Increase row)**:** Skip 1, purl across, chain increase 1 peg: 5 pegs used.

Rows 3 thru 4{8-8}: Repeat Rows 1 and 2, 1{3-3} time(s): 7{11-11} pegs used.

Row 5{9-9}: Skip 1, knit across.

Row 6{10-10}: Skip 1, purl across.

Next 4 Rows: Repeat last 2 rows twice.

Cut yarn leaving a long length to weave in later; do **not** remove stitches from pegs.

Repeat for second Cord and Ear Flap, placing tassel on peg 16{19-21} instead of first peg.

BODY
Eyelash Stripe
Holding one strand of medium weight yarn and two strands of eyelash yarn together, make a slip knot and attach to side peg.

Round 1: Working to the right and beginning with peg 1 (center of first Ear Flap), purl 4{6-6}, chain increase 8{7-9} pegs, purl 7{11-11} across second Ear Flap, chain increase 9{7-10} pegs, purl 3{5-5} across first Ear Flap: 31{36-41} pegs used.

Begin working as circular knitting.

Purl 5{5-6} rounds.

Cut both strands of eyelash yarn.

Medium Weight Stripe: Holding two strands of medium weight yarn together, knit 6{6-7} rounds.

Cut one of the strands of medium weight yarn.

Eyelash Stripe: Holding one strand of medium weight yarn and two strands of eyelash yarn together, purl 5{5-6} rounds.

Cut both strands of eyelash yarn.

Repeat last two Stripes.

Cut yarns, leaving an 18" (45.5 cm) length for sewing.

Work gathered method to remove Hat from wheel and to close top of Hat **(Figs. 20a & b, page 50)**.

TOP CORD
Make a tassel, placing loops on peg 2.

Holding two strands of medium weight yarn together, e-wrap cast on peg 1, e-wrap next peg and lift tassel loops over top, e-wrap cast on next peg: 3 pegs used.

Make I-cord for 5" (12.5 cm).

Place loop from first and last peg on center peg.

E-wap peg and lift bottom 3 loops over top loop and off peg.

Cut yarn leaving a long length for sewing and pull through remaining loop.

Sew I-cord to top of Hat.

Weave in yarn ends.

Fingerless Mitts

▬◼▢▢ EASY

Finished Size: 9" (23 cm) around hand

Sizing Note: The type of yarn that you use (whether it's soft or has more body) and the tension you have when you wrap the yarn, greatly effects your gauge and thus the finished size. Therefore, you can easily adjust the size of your mitt by the yarn you choose and your tension.

MATERIALS

Bulky Weight Brushed Acrylic Yarn
[3 ounces, 135 yards
(85 grams, 123 meters) per skein]:
   1 skein
Scrap yarn (for a marker)
26 Peg straight wheel
Knitting wheel tool
Crochet hook, size K (6.5 mm)
Yarn needle

BULKY 5

GAUGE: 10 stitches = 3¹/₂" (9 cm);
           24 rows = 4" (10 cm)

Use the diagram for the numbering system used for this pattern.

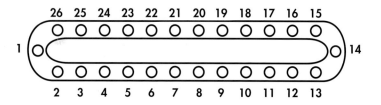

Mitts are worked using the knit stitch (instead of the e-wrap knit stitch) throughout.

THUMB

Thumb is worked as flat knitting.

Beginning with peg 23 and working on the inside of the wheel, chain cast on 9 pegs, ending on peg 5.

Row 1: Knit across.

Row 2: Purl across *(Figs. 13a-d, page 46)*.

Rows 3-6: Knit across.

Cut yarn; do **not** remove stitches from pegs.

BODY

Beginning with peg 6 and leaving a long length for sewing, chain cast on remaining pegs.

Continue to work as flat knitting across 17 Body stitches only.

Row 1: Knit across.

Row 2: Purl across.

Rows 3-6: Repeat Rows 1 and 2 twice.

Rows 7-11: Knit across.

JOIN BODY TO THUMB

Place scrap yarn around peg 6 to mark end of a round.

Begin working circular knitting.

Rounds 1-16: Knit around.

Round 17: (Knit 1, make loop stitch) around *(Figs. 14a-e, page 46)*.

Round 18: Knit around.

Round 19: (Make loop stitch, knit 1) around.

Round 20: Knit around.

Rounds 21-24: Repeat Rounds 17-20.

RIBBING

Rounds 1-3: (Knit 1, purl 1) around.

Work Ribbing bind off across all pegs *(Figs. 22a-d, page 51)*.

Sew seam along inside of Body and Thumb.

Weave in yarn ends.

Repeat for second Mitt.

Blanket Poncho

◖◼▭▭ **EASY**

Finished Size: 25{29-33}" wide x 23" long
  63.5{73.5-84} cm x 58.5 cm

Size Note: Instructions are written for adult size Small with sizes Medium and Large in braces { }. Instructions will be easier to read if you circle all the numbers pertaining to your size. If only one number is given, it applies to all sizes.

MATERIALS

BULKY 5

  Bully Weight Variegated Yarn
  [3 ounces, 111 yards
  (85 grams, 100 meters) per skein]:
    5{6-6} skeins
  62 Peg straight wheel
  Knitting wheel tool
  Crochet hook, size K (6.5 mm)
  Yarn needle

GAUGE: 9 stitches and 14 rows = 4" (10 cm)

Poncho is worked sideways as flat knitting, working fringe as you knit and using the e-wrap method for all knit stitches throughout.

FRINGE

Bring yarn to inside of wheel between last peg with loop and first empty peg, behind empty pegs and around the last empty peg to the outside of the wheel, then bring yarn along the front of the empty pegs to form a long loop ***(Fig. 2)***. Bring yarn to the inside of the wheel so that it is ready to knit the first stitch.

Fig. 2

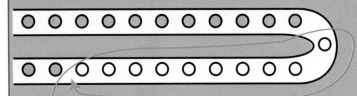

PANEL

Beginning with first peg on long side, chain cast on 52 pegs.

MOSS STITCH BORDER

Row 1: Make fringe, (knit 1, purl 1) across ***(Figs. 13a-d, page 46)***.

Row 2: (Knit 1, purl 1) across, remove fringe and let it drop to the inside of the wheel.

Rows 3-5: Repeat Rows 1 and 2 once, then repeat Row 1 once **more**.

BODY

Row 1: Knit 1, purl 1, knit 45, purl 1, (knit 1, purl 1) twice, remove fringe and let it drop to the inside of the wheel.

Row 2: Make fringe, (knit 1, purl 1) 3 times, knit 43, purl 1, knit 1, purl 1.

Repeat Rows 1 and 2 for pattern until piece measures approximately 24{28-32}"/61{71-81.5} cm from cast on edge, ending by working Row 2.

MOSS STITCH BORDER

Row 1: (Knit 1, purl 1) across, remove fringe and let it drop to the inside of the wheel.

Row 2: Make fringe, (knit 1, purl 1) across.

Rows 3-5: Repeat Rows 1 and 2 once, then repeat Row 1 once **more**.

Work chain one bind off across all pegs ***(Figs. 21a-c, page 50)***.

Repeat for second panel.

Sew panels together at shoulder seams, leaving approximately 11" (28 cm) open for neck.

Weave in yarn ends.

Double Knit Scarf

◼◼◻◻ EASY

Finished Measurement: 3½" x 55"
(9 cm x 139.5 cm)

MATERIALS

Medium Weight Variegated Yarn
MEDIUM 4
[5 ounces, 254 yards
(140 grams, 232 meters) per skein]:
  2 skeins
Small amount of waste yarn
36 Peg straight wheel
Knitting wheel tool
Crochet hook, size K (6.5 mm)
Yarn needle

GAUGE: In Body pattern,
        10 stitches and 14 rows = 3½" (9 cm)

PROVISIONAL CAST ON

See Provisional cast on, page 43.

Anchor one strand of waste yarn to side peg.

Cast on 10 sets of pegs **(Figs. 23a-d, page 52)**.

Work 3 rows in double knit.

Cut waste yarn.

BODY

Using two strands of Scarf color held together and leaving a 25" (63.5 cm) length for working the bind off, make a slip knot and attach to side peg.

> *Tip*   When wrapping the pegs, work loosely as the stitches tighten up when the bottom yarn is lifted over the pegs.

Row 1: Wrap the pegs as in Fig. 3a, then wrap the pegs as in Fig. 3b. Beginning with the last peg wrapped, lift the bottom loop on each peg over the top loop and off the peg.

Fig. 3a

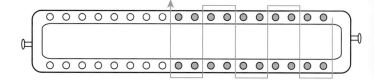

Fig. 3b

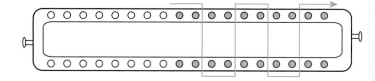

Row 2: Repeat Row 1.

Row 3: Wrap the pegs as in Fig. 3a. Work fringe across 8 pegs by wrapping the pegs as in Fig. 3c. Wrap the pegs as in Fig. 3b. Beginning with the last peg wrapped, lift the bottom loop on each peg over the top loop and off the peg.

Fig. 3c

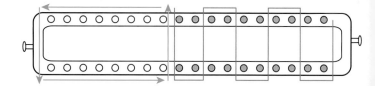

Repeat Rows 1-3 for pattern, removing fringe from pegs before working it on the next fringe row, until Scarf measures approximately 55" (139.5 cm) long **or** to desired length.

Work chain one bind off for double knit across all pegs **(Figs. 25a & b, page 54)**.

Place loops from Row 1 on pegs, removing waste yarn, and bind off using chain one bind off for double knit.

Weave in yarn ends.

12

Irish Lass Beret

■■■□ INTERMEDIATE

Finished Size: Fits most adults

Sizing Note: The type of yarn that you use (whether it's soft or has more body) and the tension you have when you wrap the yarn, greatly effects your gauge and thus the finished size. Therefore, you can easily adjust the size of your beret by the yarn you choose and your tension.

MATERIALS

Medium Weight Variegated Yarn [5 ounces, 254 yards (140 grams, 232 meters) per skein]:
   1 skein
36 Peg round wheel
Knitting wheel tool
Yarn needle

Beret is worked using two strands of yarn held together, using the e-wrap method for all knit stitches throughout.

GAUGE: 9 stitches and 12 rows = $4^1/4$" (10.75 cm)

CUFF

Cuff is worked as circular knitting.

E-wrap cast on 36 pegs.

Knit 20 rounds.

To form Cuff, lift up bottom edge toward inside of wheel and place loops from cast on row over pegs **(Fig. 18, page 49)**. Lift the bottom loop on each peg over the top loop and off the peg.

Purl 2 rounds **(Figs. 13a-d, page 46)**.

TOP WEDGES

The wedges are worked one at a time, as flat knitting, beginning by working across 6 pegs.

Increases: The Wedges will be increased by two pegs on each side. These pegs may already have a loop on them. If so, this loop will not be knitted. Instead it will be left at the bottom of the peg **(Fig. 4a)**. E-wrap the pegs to be increased, but do not bring bottom loop over top loop. When knitting the increased stitches on the following row(s), e-wrap the peg and bring the middle loop over the top loop and off the peg **(Fig. 4b)**.

Fig. 4a

Fig. 4b

Decreases: The Wedges will be decreased by one peg at the end of several rows. Move the last stitch in the wedge to the previous peg and e-wrap the same peg. If the wedge is still sharing stitches, lift middle 2 loops over top loop and off peg; otherwise lift the only 2 loops on the peg over the top loop and off peg.

FIRST WEDGE

Row 1: Knit 6, increase 2: 8 pegs used.

Row 2: Knit 8, increase 2: 10 pegs used.

Rows 3-32: Knit 10.

Row 33: Knit 8, decrease 1 peg **(Figs. 15a & b, page 47)**: 9 pegs used.

Rows 34-40: Knit across to last 2 pegs, decrease 1 peg: 2 pegs used.

Row 41: Decrease 1 peg: 1 peg used.

Cut yarn leaving a long length for sewing and pull through remaining loop on peg.

SECOND WEDGE

Row 1: Place a slip knot on the second empty peg to the left of the next stitch to count as first E-wrap, increase 1, knit 6, increase 2: 10 pegs used.

Rows 2-31: Knit 10.

Row 32: Knit 8, decrease 1 peg: 9 pegs used.

Rows 33-39: Knit across to last 2 stitches, decrease 1 peg: 2 pegs used.

Row 40: Decrease 1 peg: 1 peg used.

Cut yarn leaving a long length for sewing and pull through remaining loop on peg.

REMAINING 4 WEDGES

Work same as Second Wedge, for a total of 6 Wedges.

FINISHING

Sew Wedges together.

Weave in yarn ends.

Make a 2" (5 cm) pom-pom as follows:
Cut a piece of cardboard 3" (7.5 cm) square. Wind the yarn around the cardboard until it is approximately $1/2$" (12 mm) thick in the middle **(Fig. 5a)**. Carefully slip the yarn off the cardboard and firmly tie an 18" (45.5 cm) length of yarn around the middle **(Fig. 5b)**. Leave the ends long enough to attach the pom-pom. Cut the loops on both ends and trim the pom-pom into a smooth ball **(Fig. 5c)**.

Attach pom-pom to top of Beret.

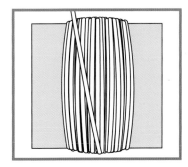

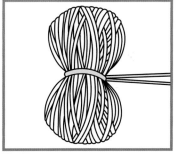

Fig. 5a   **Fig. 5b**

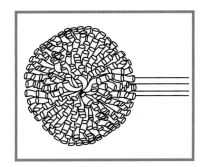

15

Corkscrew Scarf

Finished Size: 72" (183 cm) long

MATERIALS

SUPER BULKY 6

Super Bulky Weight Yarn
[1.75 ounces, 47 yards
(50 grams, 43 meters) per skein]:
   3 skeins
24 Peg round wheel or 36 peg straight wheel
Knitting wheel tool
Crochet hook, size K (6.5 mm)
Yarn needle

Gauge is not important.

SCARF

Chain cast on 5 pegs.

Scarf is worked as flat knitting, using the e-wrap method for all knit stitches throughout.

Row 1: Purl across **(Figs. 13a-d, page 46)**.

Row 2: Purl 1, knit 4.

Begin working in short rows **(Figs. 17a-c, page 48)**.

Note: When wrapping the same peg more than once, place the new wrap above the last one.

Row 3: Skip 1 **(see Skip A Peg, page 48)**, knit 2, wrap next peg.

Row 4: Knit 3.

Row 5: Skip 1, knit 1, wrap next peg.

Row 6: Knit 2.

Rows 7 and 8: Repeat Rows 5 and 6.

To knit a wrapped peg, e-wrap the next peg and lift all loops over the top loop and off the peg.

Row 9: Skip 1, knit 1, knit wrapped peg, wrap next peg.

Row 10: Knit 3.

Row 11: Skip 1, knit 2, knit wrapped peg, wrap next peg.

Row 12: Knit 4.

Row 13: Skip 1, knit 2, wrap next peg.

Row 14: Knit 3.

Row 15: Skip 1, knit 1, wrap next peg.

Row 16: Knit 2.

Rows 17 and 18: Repeat Rows 15 and 16.

Row 19: Skip 1, knit 1, knit wrapped peg, wrap next peg.

Row 20: Knit 3.

Row 21: Skip 1, knit 2, knit 2 wrapped pegs.

Repeat Rows 2-21 for pattern until Scarf measures approximately 72" (183 cm) long **or** to desired length.

Work chain one bind off across all pegs **(Figs. 21a-c, page 50)**.

Weave in yarn ends.

Adult Socks

Finished Size: 7" (18 cm) foot circumference and $7^1/2\{8^1/2\text{-}9^1/2\}$"/19{21.5-24} cm foot length

Size Note: Instructions are written for adult size 5/6 with sizes 7/8 and 9/10 in braces { }. Instructions will be easier to read if you circle all the numbers pertaining to your size. If only one number is given, it applies to all sizes.

MATERIALS

Medium Weight 100% Wool Yarn **MEDIUM 4**
[3.5 ounces, 223 yards
(100 grams, 205 meters) per skein**]**:
   1 skein
Small amount of waste yarn
26 Peg straight wheel
Knitting wheel tool
Crochet hook, size K (6.5 mm)
Yarn needle

GAUGE: 15 stitches and 23 rows = 4" (10 cm)

Use the diagram for the numbering system used for this pattern.

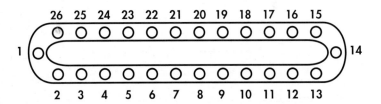

PROVISIONAL CAST ON

This Sock is a toe up pattern, that uses the provisional cast on with waste yarn **(see Provisional Cast On, page 43)**.

Begin working as flat knitting.

E-wrap cast on pegs 1-14.

E-wrap knit 3 rows.

Cut yarn and remove slip knot from side peg.

TOE SHAPING

Use the knit stitch (instead of the e-wrap knit stitch) throughout.

Anchor sock color to side peg.

Rows 1 and 2: Knit across.

Begin working in short rows **(Figs. 17a-c, page 48)**.

Row 3: Skip 1 **(see Skip A Peg, page 48)**, knit 11, wrap next peg.

Row 4: Knit 10, wrap next peg.

Row 5: Knit 9, wrap next peg.

Row 6: Knit 8, wrap next peg.

Row 7: Knit 7, wrap next peg.

Row 8: Knit 6, wrap next peg.

Row 9: Knit 5, wrap next peg.

Row 10: Knit 4, wrap next peg.

To knit a wrapped peg, e-wrap the next peg and lift all loops over the top loop and off the peg. When wrapping the same peg more than once, place the new wrap above the last one.

Row 11: Knit 4, knit wrapped peg, wrap next peg.

Row 12: Knit 5, knit wrapped peg, wrap next peg.

Row 13: Knit 6, knit wrapped peg, wrap next peg.

Row 14: Knit 7, knit wrapped peg, wrap next peg.

Row 15: Knit 8, knit wrapped peg, wrap next peg.

Row 16: Knit 9, knit wrapped peg, wrap next peg.

Row 17: Knit 10, knit wrapped peg, knit 1.

Row 18: Knit 12, knit wrapped peg, knit 1.

Row 19: Knit 13, skip the last peg.

Lift up bottom edge toward inside of wheel and place loops from first row of sock color on the pegs, placing the end stitches on pegs 1 and 14 and remaining stitches on the empty pegs **(Figs. 9a & b, page 43)**: 26 pegs used.

Remove waste yarn.

Row 20: Continuing in the same direction as the previous row, e-wrap peg 14 and lift 2 loops over top loop and off peg, knit 12.

FOOT

Begin working as circular knitting. Peg 1 is the beginning of the round.

Round 1: E-wrap peg 1 and lift 2 loops over top loop and off peg, knit around.

Knit 31{36-41} rounds.

HEEL

Begin working in short rows.

Row 1: Knit 9, wrap next peg.

Row 2: Knit 4, wrap next peg.

Row 3: Knit 4, knit wrapped peg, wrap next peg.

Row 4: Knit 5, knit wrapped peg, wrap next peg.

Row 5: Knit 6, knit wrapped peg, wrap next peg.

Row 6: Knit 7, knit wrapped peg, wrap next peg.

Row 7: Knit 8, knit wrapped peg, wrap next peg.

Row 8: Knit 9, knit wrapped peg, wrap next peg.

Row 9: Knit 10, knit wrapped peg, wrap next peg.

Row 10: Knit 11, knit wrapped peg, wrap next peg.

Row 11: Knit 12, knit wrapped peg, knit 12.

LEG

Begin working as circular knitting.

Round 1: Knit wrapped peg, purl 1, (knit 1, purl 1) around **(Figs. 13a-d, page 46)**.

Rounds 2-30: (Knit 1, purl 1) around.

Work Ribbing bind off across all pegs **(Figs. 22a-d, page 51)**.

Weave in yarn ends.

Repeat for second Sock.

Infant Socks

Finished Size: 4" (10 cm) foot circumference and
3¹/₂" (9 cm) foot length

MATERIALS

LIGHT 3

Light Weight Yarn
[5 ounces, 455 yards
(140 grams, 416 meters) per skein]:
  1 skein
Small amount of waste yarn
12 Peg round wheel
Knitting wheel tool
Yarn needle

GAUGE: 12 stitches = 4" (10 cm); 10 rows = 2" (5 cm)

PROVISIONAL CAST ON

This Sock is a toe up pattern, that uses the provisional cast on with waste yarn **(see Provisional Cast On, page 43)**.

Begin working as flat knitting.

Anchor one strand of waste yarn to side peg.

E-wrap cast on 6 pegs.

E-wrap knit 3 rows.

Cut waste yarn and remove slip knot from side peg.

TOE SHAPING

Using two strands of sock color held together, use the knit stitch (instead of the e-wrap knit stitch) throughout.

Anchor two strands of sock color to side peg.

Rows 1 and 2: Knit across.

Rows 3 and 4: Knit across, wrap next empty peg: 8 pegs used.

Begin working in short rows **(Figs. 17a-c, page 48)**.

Row 5: Knit 5, wrap next peg.

Row 6: Knit 4, wrap next peg.

Row 7: Knit 3, wrap next peg.

Row 8: Knit 2, wrap next peg.

To knit a wrapped peg, e-wrap the next peg and lift all loops over the top loop and off the peg. When wrapping the same peg more than once, place the new wrap above the last one.

Row 9: Knit 2, knit wrapped peg, wrap next peg.

Row 10: Knit 3, knit wrapped peg, wrap next peg.

Row 11: Knit 4, knit wrapped peg, wrap next peg.

Row 12: Knit 5, knit wrapped peg, wrap next peg.

Row 13: Knit 6.

Lift up bottom edge toward inside of wheel and place loops from first row of sock color on the pegs, placing the 4 center stitches on the 4 empty pegs and the end stitches on the same pegs as the first and last pegs used *(Figs. 9a & b, page 43)*: 12 pegs used.

Remove waste yarn.

Row 14: Continuing to work in the same direction as the previous row, e-wrap next peg and lift 3 loops over top loop and off peg, knit 4, e-wrap next peg and lift 3 loops over top loop and off peg.

FOOT
Begin working as circular knitting.

Knit 10 rounds.

HEEL
Begin working in short rows.

Row 1: Knit 5, wrap next peg.

Row 2: Knit 4, wrap next peg.

Row 3: Knit 3, wrap next peg.

Row 4: Knit 2, wrap next peg.

Row 5: Knit 2, knit 2 wrapped pegs, knit 6.

Row 6: Continuing to work in the same direction as the previous row, knit 2 wrapped pegs, knit 10.

LEG
Begin working as circular knitting.

Rounds 1-9: (Knit 1, purl 1) around *(Figs. 13a-d, page 46)*.

Work Ribbing bind off across all pegs *(Figs. 22a-d, page 51)*.

Weave in yarn ends.

Repeat for second Sock.

Cozy Quilt

■■■□ INTERMEDIATE

Finished Size: 30" x 36" (76 cm x 91.5 cm)

MATERIALS

Medium Weight Yarn **(4 MEDIUM)**
[16 ounces, 1,020 yards
(448 grams, 918 meters) per skein]:
  Yellow - 1 skein
  Pink - 1 skein
  Blue - 1 skein
50 Peg straight wheel
Knitting wheel tool
Crochet hook, size K (6.5 mm)
Yarn needle

Holding two strands together, wind Yellow and Pink yarn into 2 balls each.

Panels are worked using two strands of yarn held together, using the double knit method throughout **(see Double Knitting, page 52)**.

GAUGE: 8 stitches and 16 rows = 4" (10 cm)

PANEL (Make 3)

When instructed to cut a yarn, remember to leave a long length for weaving in later. New colors are always added to the inside of the wheel.

When changing colors, twist the yarns dropping the color that you are working with **over** the top of the color you will use next and to the back **(Figs. 19a & b, page 49)** and continue wrapping the stitches in the same direction as you would otherwise.

With Pink cast on 16 sets of pegs, with Yellow cast on next 4 sets of pegs: 20 sets of pegs used.

Rows 1-8: Work across using matching colors.

Row 9: Work across 8 sets of pegs using matching colors, with a second ball of Yellow work across.

Rows 10-16: Work across using matching colors.

Row 17: Work across 8 sets of pegs matching colors, cut second Yellow, with Blue work across.

Rows 18-24: Work across using matching colors.

Row 25: Cut Yellow and Pink, with Pink (at beginning of row) work across 8 sets of pegs, with Blue work across 4 sets of pegs, with Yellow work across 4 sets of pegs, with a second ball of Pink work across 4 sets of pegs.

Rows 26-32: Work across using matching colors.

Row 33: Cut first Pink, with a second ball of Yellow, work across 8 sets of pegs, using matching colors work across.

Rows 34-40: Work across using matching colors.

Row 41: Cut first Yellow and Blue, with Blue (at beginning of row) work across 12 sets of pegs, using matching colors work across.

Rows 42-48: Work across using matching colors.

Row 49: Cut all yarns, with Yellow work across 4 sets of pegs, with Pink work across.

Rows 50-144: Repeat Rows 2-49 once, then repeat Rows 2-48 once **more**.

Work chain one bind off for double knit across all pegs, using matching colors **(Figs. 25a & b, page 54)**.

Sew Panels together, placing them in the same direction.

Weave in yarn ends.

Checkered Flag Scarf

● ● ● ● ● ● ● ● ● ● ●

□■■□ INTERMEDIATE

Finished Measurement: 4" x 82" (10 cm x 208 cm)

MATERIALS

BULKY 5

Bulky Weight Yarn
[1.76 ounces, 82 yards
(50 grams, 75 meters) per skein]:
  White - 1 skein
  Black - 1 skein
26 Peg straight wheel or 31 peg round wheel
Knitting wheel tool
Crochet hook, size K (6.5 mm)
Yarn needle

GAUGE: 12 stitches = 4" (10 cm)

SCARF

Scarf is worked as flat knitting, using the knit stitch (instead of the e-wrap knit stitch).

In each row, the colors are worked in opposite directions, so that they can easily be changed at the end of each color section without cutting the yarns.

With White, chain cast on pegs 1 to 6, drop White; with Black, chain cast on pegs 12 to 7 (in reverse order). Twist the yarns where the two colors meet **(Figs. 19a & b, page 49)**.

Row 1: With White knit pegs 6 to 1; with Black knit pegs 7 to 12.

Row 2: With White knit pegs 1 to 6; with Black knit pegs 12 to 7.

Rows 3-8: Repeat Rows 1 and 2, 3 times.

Note: It may be helpful to keep track of which row you are on as you work each section, instead of counting the rows later.

White and Black yarns should be at the center of the Scarf (pegs 6 and 7 respectively). Drop White yarn over the top of the Black yarn.

Row 9: With Black knit pegs 6 to 1; with White knit pegs 7 to 12.

Row 10: With Black knit pegs 1 to 6; with White knit pegs 12 to 7.

Rows 11-16: Repeat Rows 9 and 10, 3 times.

Black and White yarns should be at the center of the Scarf. Drop Black yarn over the top of the White yarn.

Repeat Rows 1-16 for pattern until Scarf measures approximately 82" (208 cm) **or** almost to the end of the skeins, ending by working Row 16 and leaving enough yarn to bind off.

Work chain one bind off using corresponding color and working from the center to the outer edge **(Figs. 21a-c, page 50)**.

Weave in yarn ends.

Felted Fedora

INTERMEDIATE

Finished Size: Fits most children/adults; the size depends a lot on the felting process.

Size Note: Instructions are written for child size with adult size in braces { }. If only one number is given, it applies to both sizes.

MATERIALS

Medium Weight 100% Wool Yarn
[3.5 ounces, 223 yards
(100 grams, 205 meters) per skein**]**:
   Main Color - 2 skeins
   Contrasting Color - 1 skein
Small amount of scrap yarn
36{41} Peg round wheel
Knitting wheel tool
Crochet hook, size K (6.5 mm)
Yarn needle
Sewing needle and thread

Fedora is worked using two strands of yarn held together throughout.

GAUGE: 12 stitches and 18 rows = 4" (10 cm)

BRIM

Ribbing is worked across 5 pegs with a sixth peg used to create loops that will be tied together in two's with scrap yarn so that they can later be placed on the wheel to start the Body. The ends of the Brim will be joined together forming a circle.

The Brim is worked as a flat knitting, using the e-wrap method for all knit stitches.

Holding 2 strands of main color together, e-wrap cast on 6 pegs.

Row 1: Skip 1 *(see Skip A Peg, page 48)*, knit 1, (purl 1, knit 1) twice *(Figs. 13a-d, page 46)*.

Row 2: Knit 1, (purl 1, knit 1) twice, e-wrap end peg but do not knit it.

Row 3: Skip 1, K1, (purl 1, knit 1) twice.

Row 4: Knit 1, (purl 1, knit 1) twice; bring a piece of scrap yarn through the 2 loops on the last peg and tie ends together *(Fig. 6a)*, remove loops from the peg and let them drop to the inside of the wheel *(Fig. 6b)*; e-wrap empty peg.

Fig. 6a

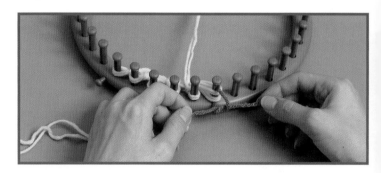

Fig. 6b

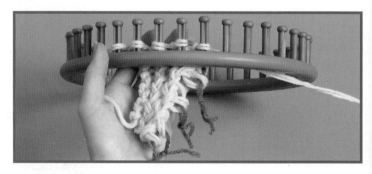

Repeat Rows 1-4, 35{40} times, ending last row by not e-wrapping empty peg.

To join ends to form a circle, lift up the bottom edge toward inside of wheel and place the first 5 cast on loops on the corresponding peg (not the tied loops). Lift the bottom loop on each peg over the top loop and off the peg.

Bind off using chain one bind off.

BODY

To attach the Brim to the wheel, bring the tied loops up through the inside of the wheel, and twisting each loop set, place them on a peg; remove waste yarn.

26

Holding one strand of main color and one strand of contrasting color together, make a slip knot and attach to side peg.

Begin working as circular knitting, continuing to use e-wrap method for all knit stitches throughout.

Round 1: Knit around, lifting loops from Brim over top loop and off pegs.

Purl 7 rounds.

Cut contrasting color leaving a long length to weave in later.

Holding two strands of main color together, knit 22{26} rounds.

Cut yarn leaving a 18" (45.5 cm) length.

Work gathered method to remove Hat from wheel and to close top of Hat *(Figs. 20a & b, page 50)*.

Weave in all yarn ends.

Felt and shape *(see Felting, page 55)*.

Make Felted Flower, page 28, and sew to Fedora.

Felted Flower

Shown on page 27.

●▮▮▯ INTERMEDIATE

MATERIALS

Medium Weight 100% Wool Yarn
[3.5 ounces, 223 yards
(100 grams, 205 meters) per skein]:
 a small amount of 2 colors
Round or straight wheel with at least 7 pegs
Knitting wheel tool
Crochet hook, size K (6.5 mm)
Yarn needle

Gauge is not important.

If you're using a knitting wheel with large pegs, use two strands of yarn held together throughout, otherwise only use one strand.

FLOWER

Flower is worked as flat knitting, using the e-wrap method for all knit stitches throughout.

E-wrap cast on 3 pegs.

Row 1: Knit across.

Row 2 (Increase row)**:** Knit across, e-wrap increase 1 peg **(Fig. 16, page 48)**: 4 pegs used.

Begin working in short rows **(Figs. 17a-c, page 48)**.

Row 3: Knit across to last peg used, wrap last peg.

Row 4 (Increase row)**:** Knit across, e-wrap increase 1 peg: 5 pegs used.

Note: You will be wrapping the same peg each time, placing the new wrap above the last one.

Rows 5-8: Repeat Rows 3 and 4 twice: 7 pegs used.

Row 9: Knit across to last peg, e-wrap last peg and lift 4 loops over top loop and off peg.

Rows 10 and 11: Knit across.

Row 12 (Decrease row)**:** Decreasing last peg **(Figs. 15a & b, page 47)**, knit across: 6 pegs used.

Row 13: Knit across to last peg, wrap last peg.

Rows 14-18: Repeat Rows 12 and 13 twice, then repeat Row 12 once **more**: 3 pegs used.

Row 19: Knit across to last peg, e-wrap last peg and lift 4 loops over top loop and off peg.

Row 20: Knit across.

Rows 21-60: Repeat Rows 1-20 twice for a total of 3 petals.

To form a circle, lift up the bottom edge toward inside of wheel and place loops from cast on row on the used pegs **(Fig. 18, page 49)**. Lift the bottom loop on each peg over the top loop and off the peg.

Work chain one bind off **(Figs. 21a-c, page 50)**; cut yarn leaving a 20" (51 cm) length for sewing.

Thread yarn needle with end and weave through center of Flower; pull yarn to tighten and secure end.

Weave in yarn ends.

Make a second Flower using a contrasting color.

Felt both Flowers **(see Felting, page 55)**.

Sew Flowers together at center, using color of bottom Flower.

Felted Wallet Belt

Shown on page 31.

◼◼◼▢ **INTERMEDIATE**

Finished Size: 2" wide x 38{42-48}" long (belt) **[**5 cm x 96.5{106.5-122} cm**]** after felting

Size Note: Instructions are written for adult size Small with sizes Medium and Large in braces { }. Instructions will be easier to read if you circle all the numbers pertaining to your size. If only one number is given, it applies to all sizes.

MATERIALS

Medium Weight 70% Wool Variegated Yarn **MEDIUM 4** **[**2.8 ounces, 110 yards (80 grams, 100 meters) per skein**]**:
    2 skeins
38 Peg straight wheel
Knitting wheel tool
Crochet hook, size K (6.5 mm)
Adjustable belt buckle for 2" (5 cm) wide belt
Magnetic clasp
Yarn needle
Optional flat sided bead and glue

GAUGE: 10 stitches and 16 rows = 4" (10 cm)

Use the diagram for the numbering system used for this pattern.

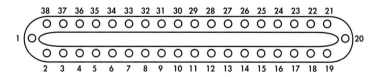

Bottom of Wallet is worked as flat knitting, using the e-wrap method for all knit stitches throughout.

WALLET BOTTOM

Chain cast on pegs 1 to 20.

Row 1: Knit across.

Begin working in short rows *(Figs. 17a-c, page 48)*.

Row 2: Skip 1 *(see Skip A Peg, page 48)*, knit 18, wrap next peg.

Rows 3-5: Knit 18, wrap next peg.

Row 6: Knit 18.

Lift up bottom edge toward inside of wheel and place cast on loops on the empty pegs, placing the end stitches on the same pegs as the first and last pegs used; e-wrap next peg (peg 20) and lift 3 loops over top loop and off peg, continuing to work in the same direction, knit 18: 38 pegs used.

SIDES

Begin working as circular knitting.

Round 1: E-wrap next peg (peg 1) and lift 3 loops over top loop and off peg, knit around.

Knit 21 rounds.

Chain one bind off peg 1, then 38 to 20 *(Figs. 21a-c, page 50)*; place loop from crochet hook on next peg (peg 19).

Instructions continued on page 30.

FLAP

Begin flat knitting across remaining 18 stitches.

Row 1: E-wrap next peg (peg 19) and lift 2 loops over top loop and off peg, knit across.

Rows 2-6: Skip 1, knit 17.

Rows 7-22: Decreasing first peg, knit across: 2 pegs used.

Row 23: Decrease.

Cut yarn and pull through loop on crochet hook.

BELT
LONG SIDE

Chain cast on 10 pegs.

Work as flat knitting.

Row 1: Knit across.

Row 2: Purl across.

Repeat Rows 1 and 2 until Belt measures approximately 29{32-35}"/73.5{81.5-89} cm, ending by working Row 1.

Next Row (Increase row)**:** Purl across; chain increase 1 peg: 11 pegs used.

Next Row: Knit across.

Repeat last 2 rows, 3 times: 14 pegs used.

Work chain one bind off across all pegs.

SHORT SIDE

Chain cast on 10 pegs.

Work as flat knitting.

Row 1: Knit across.

Row 2: Purl across.

Repeat Rows 1 and 2 until Belt measures approximately 4{5-8}"/10{12.5-20.5} cm, ending by working Row 1.

Next Row (Increase row)**:** Purl across; chain increase 1 peg: 11 pegs used.

Next Row: Knit across.

Repeat last 2 rows, 3 times: 14 pegs used.

Work chain one bind off across all pegs.

Using diagram as guide for placement, sew ends of Belt to Wallet.

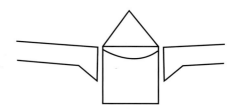

Sew hole in bottom of Wallet. Weave in yarn ends.

Felt Bag **(see Felting, page 55)**.

Slip buckle onto end of Short Belt, fold over 1¹/₂" (4 cm) and sew in place.
Attach magnetic clasp, according to package directions, to Wallet Flap.
Glue on bead if desired.

Felted Slippers

INTERMEDIATE

Size Note: Instructions are written for child size with adult size in braces { }. If only one number is given, it applies to both sizes.

MATERIALS

Medium Weight 100% Wool Yarn
[3.5 ounces, 223 yards
(100 grams, 205 meters) per skein]:
  2 skeins
24{31} Peg round wheel
Knitting wheel tool
Crochet hook, size K (6.5 mm)
Yarn needle

Slippers are worked using two strands of yarn held together, using the e-wrap method for all knit stitches throughout.

GAUGE: 10 stitches and 12 rows = 4" (10 cm)

CUFF

Begin working flat knitting.

Working on the inside of the wheel, chain cast on all pegs.

Knit 12{16} rows.

Continuing in the same direction as previous row, begin working as circular knitting.

Knit 2{4} rounds.

HEEL SHAPING

Begin working in short rows *(Figs. 17a-c, page 48)*.

Row 1: Knit 18{23}, wrap next peg.

Note: When wrapping the same peg more than once, place the new wrap above the last one.

Rows 2-4: Knit 12{15}, wrap next peg.

Row 5: Knit 11{14}, wrap next peg.

Rows 6-8: Knit 10{13}, wrap next peg.

Row 9: Knit 9{12}, wrap next peg.

Rows 10-12: Knit 8{11}, wrap next peg.

Row 13: Knit 7{10}, wrap next peg.

Rows 14-16: Knit 6{9}, wrap next peg.

Row 17: Knit 5{8}, wrap next peg.

Rows 18-20: Knit 4{7}, wrap next peg.

Adult Size Only

Row 21: Knit 6, wrap next peg.

Rows 22-24: Knit 5, wrap next peg.

FOOT

Begin working as circular knitting.

Round 1: Working in opposite direction of previous row, knit 4{5}, e-wrap next 5{6} pegs and lift 3 loops over top loop and off peg, knit 10{14}, e-wrap next 5{6} pegs and lift the bottom 3 loops on each peg over the top loop and off the peg, knit around.

Knit 22{27} rounds.

Cut yarn leaving a 18" (45.5 cm) length.

Work gathered method to remove Slipper from wheel and to close toe *(Figs. 20a & b, page 50)*.

Weave in yarn ends.
Repeat for second Slipper.

Felt and shape *(see Felting, page 55)*.

● ● ● ● INTERMEDIATE

Size	Bust	Finished Bust Measurement
X-Small	28/30	32" (81.5 cm)
Small	32/34	36¹/₂" (92.5 cm)
Medium	36/38	40" (101.5 cm)
Large	40/42	44¹/₂" (113 cm)
X-Large	44/46	48" (122 cm)

Size Note: Instructions are written for adult size X-Small and Small in first set of braces { }, with sizes Medium, Large, and X-Large in second set. Instructions will be easier to read if you circle all the numbers pertaining to your size. If only one number is given, it applies to all sizes.

MATERIALS

Bully Weight Yarn
[3 ounces, 123 yards
(85 grams, 113 meters) per skein]:
  {7-7}{8-9-10} skeins
Scrap yarn (for a marker)
62 Peg straight wheel
Knitting wheel tool
Crochet hook, size K (6.5 mm)
Yarn needle

GAUGE: 11 stitches and 18 rows = 4" (10 cm)

The Back and Fronts are worked from side-to-side. Therefore the number of the pegs used is the length of the sweater and the number of rows worked is the width. The Sleeves are worked up from the Ribbing. Stitch **and** row gauge is very important. Be sure to make a gauge swatch.

Sweater is worked as flat knitting using the e-wrap method for all knit stitches throughout.

RIBBING PATTERN

The Ribbing pattern is worked across the bottom of the sweater using 17 pegs. A yarn marker is used to mark peg 17 as a reminder to start Ribbing on even-numbered pattern rows. Row 1 and all odd-numbered pattern rows begin at bottom edge of Sweater. Keep track of which row you have worked.

Row 1: Knit 5, purl 2 *(Figs. 13a-d, page 46)*, knit 4, purl 2, knit 4.
Row 2: Knit 4, purl 2, knit 4, purl 2, knit 5.
Rows 3-6: Repeat Rows 1 and 2 twice.
Row 7: Knit 1, purl 4, (knit 2, purl 4) twice.
Row 8: Purl 4, (knit 2, purl 4) twice, knit 1.
Rows 9 and 10: Repeat Rows 1 and 2.
Repeat Rows 1-10 for pattern.

BACK

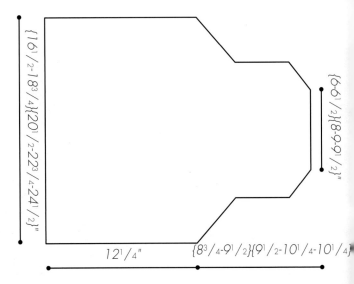

{16¹/₂-18³/₄}{20¹/₂-22³/₄-24¹/₂}"

{6-6¹/₂}{8-9-9¹/₂}"

12¹/₄"   {8³/₄-9¹/₂}{9¹/₂-10¹/₄-10¹/₄"

Holding the wheel with the outer edge facing you *(Fig. 8e, page 42)* and beginning at the third peg from the left hand end, chain cast on 17 pegs, place scrap yarn around next peg, chain cast on same peg and on next 16 pegs: 34 pegs used.

Row 1: Work Row 1 of Ribbing pattern, knit across.

Row 2: Knit across to marker, work next row of Ribbing pattern.

Row 3 (Increase row)**:** Work next row of Ribbing pattern, knit across, chain increase 1 peg *(see Chain Increase, page 48)*: 35 pegs used.

Row 4: Knit across to marker, work next row of Ribbing pattern.

Rows 5-18: Repeat Rows 3 and 4, 7 times: 42 pegs used.

Row 19: Work next row of Ribbing pattern, knit across, chain increase {12-14}{14-16-16} pegs for armholes: {54-56}{56-58-58} pegs used.

Rows 20-28: Repeat Rows 2 and 3, 4 times; then repeat Row 2 once **more**: {58-60}{60-62-62} pegs used.

Row 29: Work next row of Ribbing pattern, knit across.

Row 30: Knit across to marker, work next row of Ribbing pattern.

Rows 31 thru {48-58}{66-76-84}: Repeat Rows 29 and 30, {9–14}{18-23-27} times.

Row {49-59}{67-77-85} (Decrease row)**:** Work next row of Ribbing pattern, knit across to last 4 pegs, decrease one stitch 3 stitches in by moving the loops from the last 3 pegs over so that 2 loops are on the next peg and one loop is on each of the last 2 pegs *(Fig. 15c, page 47)*, knit remaining stitches: {57-59}{59-61-61} pegs used.

Row {50-60}{68-78-86}: Knit across to marker, work next row of Ribbing pattern.

Rows {51-61}{69-79-87} thru {56-66}{74-84-92}: Repeat last 2 rows, 3 times: {54-56}{56-58-58} pegs used.

Row {57-67}{75-85-93}: Work next row of Ribbing pattern, knit across.

Row {58-68}{76-86-94}: Chain one bind off next {12-14}{14-16-16} pegs for armholes *(Figs. 21a-c, page 50)*, place loop from crochet hook onto next peg with a loop, e-wrap next peg and lift 2 loops over top loop and off peg, knit across to marker, work next row of Ribbing pattern: 42 pegs used.

Row {59-69}{77-87-95} (Decrease row)**:** Work next row of Ribbing pattern, knit across to last 4 pegs, decrease one stitch, knit remaining stitches: 41 pegs used.

Row {60-70}{78-88-96}: Knit across to marker, work next row of Ribbing pattern.

Rows {61-71}{79-89-97} thru {74-84}{92-102-110}: Repeat last 2 rows, 7 times: 34 pegs used.

Work chain one bind off across all pegs.

LEFT FRONT

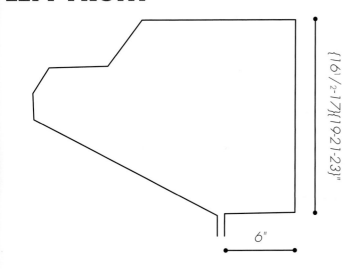

Holding the wheel with the outer edge facing you and beginning at the eighteen peg from the right hand end, chain cast on 4 pegs; make I-cord for {26-28}{30-32-34}"/{66-71}{76-81.5-86.5} cm *(see I-cord, page 54)*.

Row 1: Knit 4 (from left to right), place scrap yarn around next peg, chain increase 17 pegs: 21 pegs used.

Row 2 (Increase row): Work Row 1 of Ribbing pattern, knit across, chain increase 1 peg: 22 pegs used.

Sizes Medium, Large and X-Large Only

Row 3: Knit across to marker, work next row of Ribbing pattern.

Row 4 (Increase row): Work next row of Ribbing pattern, knit across, chain increase 1 peg: 23 pegs used.

Rows 5 thru {22-34-54}: Repeat Rows 3 and 4, {9-15-25} times: {32-38-48} pegs used.

All Sizes

Row {3-3}{23-35-55}: Knit across to marker, work next row of Ribbing pattern.

Row {4-4}{24-36-56} (Increase row): Work next row of Ribbing pattern, knit across, chain increase 2 pegs: {24-24}{34-40-50} pegs used.

Row {5-5}{25-37-57}: Knit across to marker, work next row of Ribbing pattern.

Rows {6-6}{26-38-58} thru {39-41}{51-59-69}: Repeat last 2 rows, {17-18}{13-11-6} times: {58-60}{60-62-62} pegs used.

Row {40-42}{52-60-70}: Work next row of Ribbing pattern, knit across.

Row {41-43}{53-61-71}: Knit across to marker, work next row of Ribbing pattern.

Rows {42-44}{54-62-72} thru {47-49}{59-67-77}: Repeat last 2 rows, 3 times.

Row {48-50}{60-68-78} (Decrease row): Work next row of Ribbing pattern, knit across to last 4 pegs, decrease one stitch, knit remaining stitches: {57-59}{59-61-61} pegs used.

Row {49-51}{61-69-79}: Knit across to marker, work next row of Ribbing pattern.

Rows {50-52}{62-70-80} thru {55-57}{67-75-85}: Repeat last 2 rows, 3 times: {54-56}{56-58-58} pegs used.

Instructions continued on page 38.

Row {56-58}{68-76-86}: Work next row of Ribbing pattern, knit across.

Row {57-59}{69-77-87}: Chain one bind off next {12-14}{14-16-16} pegs for armholes, place loop on crochet hook on next peg with a loop, e-wrap next peg and lift 2 loops over top loop and off peg, knit across to marker, work next row of Ribbing pattern: 42 pegs used.

Row {58-60}{70-78-88} (Decrease row)**:** Work next row of Ribbing pattern, knit across to last 4 pegs, decrease one stitch, knit remaining stitches: 41 pegs used.

Row {59-61}{71-79-89}: Knit across to marker, work next row of Ribbing pattern.

Rows {60-62}{72-80-90} thru {74-76}{86-94-104}: Repeat last 2 rows, 7 times: 34 pegs used.

Work chain one bind off across all pegs.

RIGHT FRONT

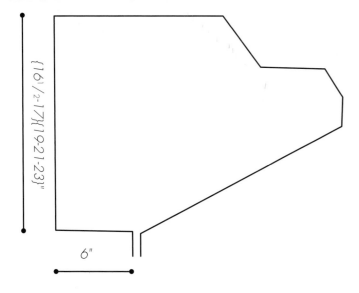

Holding the wheel with the outer edge facing you and beginning at the tenth peg from the right hand end, chain cast on 4 pegs; make I-cord for 10" (25.5 cm).

Row 1: Work one more row of I-cord, place scrap yarn around next peg (to left of cord), chain increase 17 pegs: 21 pegs used.

Beginning with Row 2, work same as Left Front.

SLEEVE (Make 2)

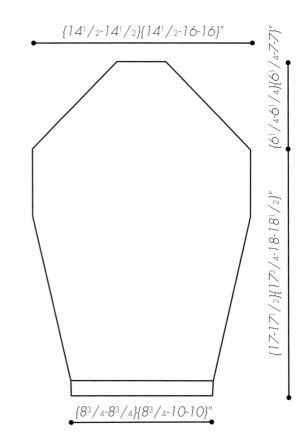

RIBBING

Holding the wheel with the outer edge facing you and beginning at the {12-12}{12-14-14} peg from the left hand end, chain cast on {24-24}{24-28-28} pegs.

Row 1: (Knit 2, purl 2) across.

Row 2: (Purl 2, knit 2) across.

Rows 3-5: Repeat Rows 1 and 2 once, then repeat Row 1 once **more**.

BODY

Rows 1-5: Knit across.

Row 6 (Increase row)**:** Chain increase 1 peg, knit across, chain increase 1 peg: {26-26}{26-30-30} pegs used.

Rows 7-48: Repeat Rows 1-6, 7 times: {40-40}{40-44-44} pegs used.

Knit {23-25}{27-29-31} rows.

CAP

Row 1 (Decrease row)**:** Decrease 3 stitches in by moving the loops from the first 3 pegs over so that 2 loops are on the third peg and one loop is on each of the first 2 pegs, knit across to last 4 pegs, decrease one stitch, knit remaining stitches: {38-38}{38-42-42} pegs used.

Row 2: Knit across.

Rows 3-16: Repeat Rows 1 and 2, 7 times: {24-24}{24-28-28} pegs used.

Row 17 (Decrease row)**:** Decrease one stitch on each edge by moving the loop from the first and last pegs over to the next peg, knit across: {22-22}{22-26-26} pegs used.

Row 18: Knit across.

Repeat Rows 17 and 18, {5-5}{5-7-7} times: 12 pegs used.

Work chain one bind off across all pegs.

FINISHING

Sew shoulder seams using backstitch and leaving center {6-6^1/$_2$}{8-9-9^1/$_2$}"/{15-16.5}{20.5-23-24} cm for neck.
Sew Sleeve Cap to sweater, matching center of last row on Sleeve to shoulder seam.
Sew underarm and side in one continuous seam, leaving a 1" (2.5 cm) opening along right side, approximately 7^1/$_2$" (19 cm) from bottom edge for the long tie to go through.

SYMBOLS AND TERMS

★ – work instructions following ★ as many **more** times as indicated in addition to the first time.

( ) or **[ ]** – work enclosed instructions **as many** times as specified by the number immediately following **or** contains explanatory remarks.

colon (:) – the number(s) given after a colon at the end of a row or round denote(s) the number of pegs used you should have on that row or round.

working yarn – the strand coming from the skein

Yarn Weight Symbol & Names	SUPER FINE 1	FINE 2	LIGHT 3	MEDIUM 4	BULKY 5	SUPER BULKY 6
Type of Yarns in Category	Sock, Fingering Baby	Sport, Baby	DK, Light Worsted	Worsted, Afghan, Aran	Chunky, Craft, Rug	Bulky, Roving
Knit Gauge Ranges in Stockinette St to 4" (10 cm)	27-32 sts	23-26 sts	21-24 sts	16-20 sts	12-15 sts	6-11 sts
Advised Needle Size Range	1-3	3-5	5-7	7-9	9-11	11 and larger

GAUGE

Exact gauge is essential for specified size of project. Before beginning your project, make a sample swatch with the yarn and wheel specified in the individual instructions. After completing the swatch, give it a tug, holding the cast on and bound off edges, then let it "rest". Measure it, counting your stitches and rows carefully. If your swatch is larger or smaller than specified, make another, changing your tension. Keep trying until you find the tension you need to achieve gauge. Maintain established gauge throughout project.

WRAPPING THE YARN

Producing knit fabric on the round wheel and straight wheel involves wrapping the yarn around the pegs. It is absolutely essential to wrap the yarn loose enough to be able to lift it off the peg, but not so loose that it falls off. As you wrap, let the yarn gently slide through your hand.

Tip If you are holding more that one strand of yarn together, be sure to treat them as one.

CASTING ON

The initial wrap of the wheel is called the **"cast on row."** The simplest cast on method for wheel knitting is referred to as **"e-wrap"** and is worked the same as the first half of the e-wrap knit stitch. The **"chain stitch"** cast on method produces a tighter cast on row with a more finished look than the e-wrap cast on. The **"provisional"** cast on method is used to keep stitches "live" so that the stitches in the first row of your project can be used again. Use the e-wrap cast on using a different color yarn than your project.

When instructed to **anchor yarn**, attach the end of the yarn to the side peg with a slip knot **(Figs. 27a-c, page 55)**. This holds the beginning yarn and also the working yarn until you are ready to use it.

E-WRAP CAST ON

Leaving a 6" (15 cm) end, insert the yarn end into the center of the wheel from the top to the bottom, and anchor yarn **(Fig. 7a)**. Once the anchored yarn is removed, the yarn end will hang to the inside of the wheel.

Fig. 7a

Holding the wheel however it is most comfortable to you, wrap the yarn around the first peg (to the right of the anchored yarn) in a clockwise direction, ending at the inside of the wheel **(Fig. 7b)**. Moving around the wheel to your right and wrapping each peg **loosely**, wrap the next peg clockwise, ending at the inside. Continue around, turning the wheel every few wraps, and pushing the loops down with your other hand as you go until all of the pegs have been wrapped that you need for the project that you are making **(Fig. 7c)**.

Tip As you push the loops down, leave your finger on the last loop to prevent it from falling off.

Fig. 7b   **Fig. 7c**

Tip The yarn should cross at the inside of the wheel **(Fig. 7d)**, leaving a loop on the outside of each peg **(Fig. 7e)**.

Fig. 7d   **Fig. 7e**

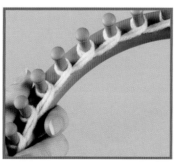 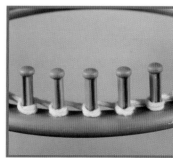

CHAIN CAST ON

Leaving a 6" (15 cm) end, put a slip knot on the crochet hook.

In order for the next row to be worked from right to left, you will need to work on the inside of the wheel also holding the crochet hook to the inside. Wrap the working yarn around the back of the first peg and bring it to the inside *(Fig. 8a)*.

Fig. 8a

Lay the working yarn on top of the crochet hook with the peg being encircled by the yarn. Catching the working yarn with the hook, bring it through the loop that is on the crochet hook, producing a chain stitch with the peg in the middle of the chain stitch *(Fig. 8b)*.

Fig. 8b

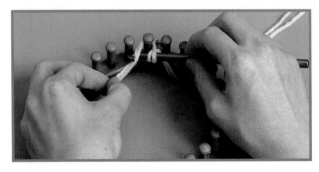

The resulting loop on the hook should be large enough to easily reach the next peg *(Fig. 8c)*.

Fig. 8c

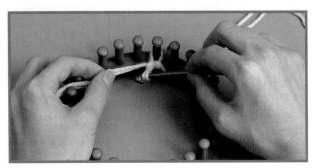

★ For the next cast on stitch, wrap the working yarn around the back of the next peg and bring it to the inside, lay the working yarn on top of the crochet hook, and bring it through the loop that is on the crochet hook.

Repeat from ★ until you have cast on one peg less than needed.

For the last cast on stitch, keep the working yarn to the inside of the wheel and place the loop that is on the crochet hook on the next peg *(Fig. 8d)*.

Fig. 8d

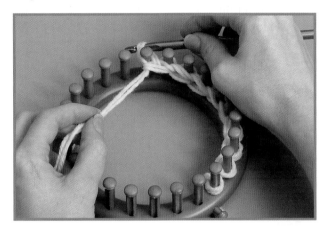

When you are instructed to cast on in reverse order or for the next row to be worked from left to right, you will need to hold the wheel with the outer edge facing you and the crochet hook to the inside. Work the same as before, only wrapping the yarn around the front of the pegs *(Fig. 8e)*.

Fig. 8e

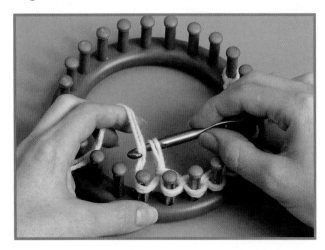

PROVISIONAL CAST ON

A provisional cast on is just a temporary cast on, using a different color yarn than your project, referred to as *"waste yarn."* It is used on the Socks. After a few inches have been knit, the first row of stitches are hung on the empty pegs so that these loops can be knitted, forming the toe. It is also used for the Double Knit Scarf to establish the pattern, and then to allow the beginning end to be bound off.

When you are instructed to place loops from the first row of main color on the pegs, lift up the bottom edge toward inside of wheel **(Fig. 9a)**. The red circle shows which loop of the main color yarn you will put on a peg. Beginning with the end stitch, place each loop from first row of main color on the pegs specified in the instructions **(Fig. 9b)**.

> *Tip* Pulling the waste yarn from each stitch as you put it on a peg works very well. Work carefully so that you do not unravel the first row of the main color.

Fig. 9a

Fig. 9b

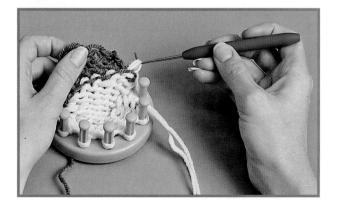

KNIT STITCH

There are two ways to make a knit stitch. The *"e-wrap"* knit stitch is a twisted stitch. The following method is a "true" knit stitch and is a smaller stitch than the e-wrap knit stitch. The instructions will specify which method to use.

Step 1: Loosely lay the working yarn on the outside of the wheel, above the loops that are already on the pegs **(Fig. 10a)**.

Fig. 10a

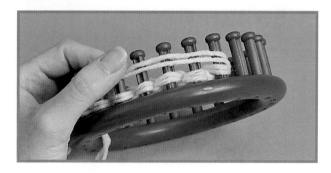

Step 2: Using the tool, lift the bottom loop over the working yarn and off the peg, allowing the yarn to curve around the front half of the peg **(Fig. 10b)**.

Fig. 10b

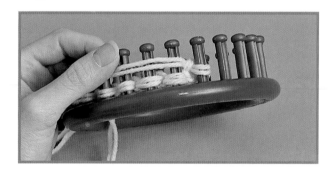

Repeat Steps 1 and 2 for each peg to be knitted.

Note: This knit stitch is worked the same for flat and circular knitting on both the round wheel and the straight wheel. After working 3 or 4 rows or rounds, remove the anchored yarn from the side peg and allow the bottom of the piece to hang free.

The right side of the piece hangs towards the outside of the wheel (**Figs. 10c & d**).

Fig. 10c   right side

Fig. 10d   wrong side

E-WRAP KNIT STITCH

When working **circularly**, the pegs are always wrapped in the same direction. When working **flat** (back and forth in rows), the pegs are wrapped in the opposite direction on each row.

Each project that uses the e-wrap method for all knit stitches will have it stated at the beginning of the instructions. Then the instructions will simply instruct you to knit the required number of stitches.

CIRCULAR KNITTING

Step 1 (Wrapping row): When knitting circularly, making a tubular project, continue around the wheel in the same direction as the cast on, wrapping the pegs clockwise a second time until all of the pegs have 2 loops on them, again pushing the loops down as you go (**Fig. 11a**).

Fig. 11a

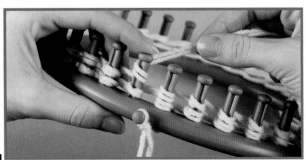

Step 2 (Completing knit stitches)**:** Using the tool, lift the bottom loop on the last peg wrapped over the top loop and off the peg (**Fig. 11b**). This completes the e-wrap knit stitch and secures the working yarn. Continue around until there is one loop on each peg, working in either direction.

Fig. 11b

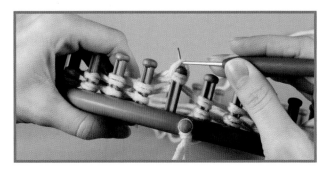

For each of the following rounds, wrap each peg clockwise, ending at the inside of the wheel (2 loops on each peg). Then, complete the knit stitches.

Note: After working 3 or 4 rounds, remove the anchored yarn from the side peg and allow the bottom of the piece to hang free.

The right side of the piece hangs towards the outside of the wheel (**Figs. 11c & d**).

Fig. 11c   right side

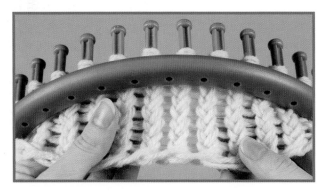

Fig. 11d   wrong side

FLAT KNITTING

To create a flat piece, work back and forth in rows, either on the round wheel or the straight wheel. Cast on the number of pegs according to the instructions. All or only some of the pegs may be used.

Step 1: Wrap the last peg worked clockwise **(Fig. 12a)**, then working to your left, wrap each peg counter-clockwise until all of the pegs have 2 loops on them **(Fig. 12b)**.

Fig. 12a   **Fig. 12b**

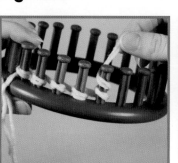   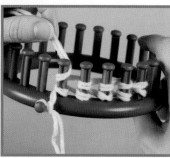

Step 2: Using the tool and beginning with the last peg wrapped **(Fig. 12c)**, lift the bottom loop on each peg over the top loop and off the peg, completing the e-wrap knit stitches **(Fig. 12d)**.

Fig. 12c   **Fig. 12d**

   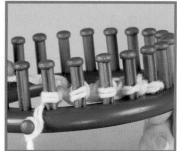

Step 3 (Wrapping row)**:** Wrap the first peg counter-clockwise **(Fig.12e)**, then working to your right, wrap each remaining peg clockwise **(Fig. 12f)**.

Fig. 12e   **Fig. 12f**

Step 4 (Completing knit stitches)**:** Using the tool and beginning with the last peg wrapped, lift the bottom loop on each peg over the top loop and off the peg.

Step 5 (Wrapping row)**:** Wrap the first peg clockwise, then working to your left, wrap each remaining peg counter-clockwise.

Step 6 (Completing knit stitches)**:** Using the tool and beginning with the last peg wrapped, lift the bottom loop on each peg over the top loop and off the peg.

> *Tip*   There is an easy way to remember which direction to wrap the pegs each row. The first peg is wrapped in the same direction as the last stitch on the previous row. The remaining pegs are wrapped in the opposite direction as the first peg.

Repeat Steps 3-6, ending by working Step 4 or 6.

Note: After working 3 or 4 rows, remove the anchored yarn from the side peg and allow the bottom of the piece to hang free.

PURL STITCH

Step 1: Lay the working yarn on the outside of the wheel, **below** the loops that are already on the pegs **(Fig. 13a)**.

Fig. 13a

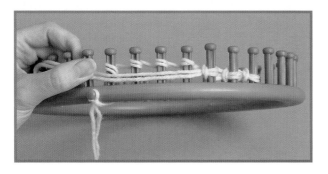

Step 2: Insert the tool down through the loop on the peg (from top to bottom) **(Fig. 13b)** and with the tip of the tool over the working yarn, pull the working yarn up through the loop forming a new loop **(Fig. 13c)**.

Fig. 13b

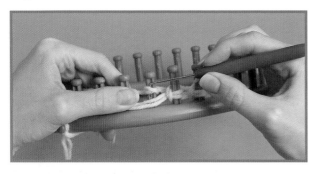

Fig. 13c

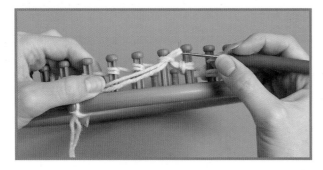

Step 3: Lift the original loop off the peg and place the newly formed loop on the peg **(Fig. 13d)**. Tighten the loop by gently pulling the working yarn, allowing the yarn to curve around the front half of the peg.

Fig. 13d

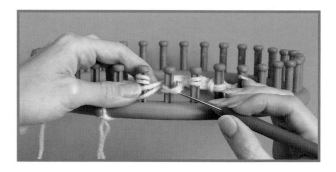

Repeat Steps 1-3 for each peg to be purled.

LOOP STITCH

The Loop stitch adds a loop within a knit stitch.

Step 1: Loosely wrap the peg 3 times **(Fig. 14a)**.

Fig. 14a

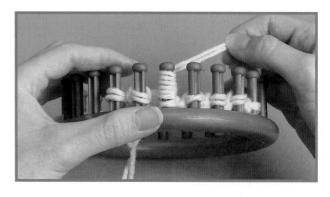

Step 2: Using the tool, lift the bottom loop over the top 3 wraps and off the peg **(Fig. 14b)**.

Fig. 14b

Step 3: Using the tool, lift the top loop of the wrap off the peg and allow the second wrap to come off also, which will elongate the wrap into a loop *(Fig. 14c)*. Bring the long loop to the right side of the peg and hold in place *(Fig. 14d)*.

Fig. 14c

Fig. 14d

Step 4: E-wrap the same peg once and lift the bottom loop over the top loop and off the peg. E-wrap the peg again and lift the bottom loop over the top loop to secure the loop stitch.

Step 5: Pull the loop to the inside of the wheel and let it dangle between the wheel and the knitting *(Fig. 14e)*.

Fig. 14e

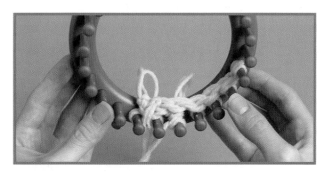

Repeat Steps 1-5 for each loop stitch.

E-WRAP DECREASES

When decreasing the first or last stitch, use the tool to move the loop from the side to be decreased to the peg one stitch in, leaving an empty peg *(Fig. 15a)*. E-wrap the same peg, then lift the bottom 2 loops over the top loop and off the peg *(Fig. 15b)*. You will have one less peg being used for each decrease made.

Fig. 15a

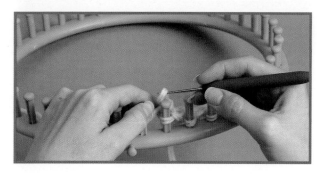

Fig. 15b

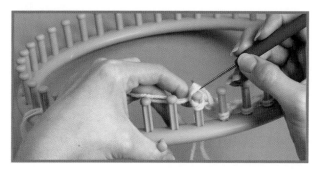

When the decrease occurs 3 stitches in from the edge, you will have to move 3 loops one at a time so that there are no empty pegs between the stitches. Begin by moving the loop on the third peg over to the fourth peg *(Fig. 15c)*, then move the loops from the end 2 pegs over so that 2 loops are on the third peg in and one loop is on each of the last 2 pegs. E-wrap the peg with 2 loops, then lift the bottom 2 loops over the top loop and off the peg.

Fig. 15c

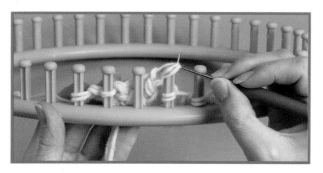

INCREASES
E-WRAP INCREASE

On the wrapping row, wrap the empty peg twice on the side of the work to be increased *(Fig. 16)*. Complete the knit stitch by lifting the bottom loop over the top loop and off the peg. You will have one more peg being used for each increase made.

Fig. 16

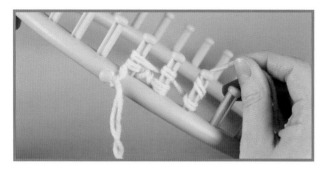

CHAIN INCREASE

Remove the last loop made from the peg and place it on the crochet hook. Follow the instructions for chain cast on, page 42, for each increase indicated in the pattern, then place the loop that is on the crochet hook on the next empty peg.

For example, if the pattern indicates to chain increase one peg, remove the loop from the peg and place it on the crochet hook, chain cast on to this peg, then place the loop from the crochet hook on the next empty peg.

SKIP A PEG

Skipping a peg gives the same result as slipping a stitch in hand knitting. When shaping an ear flap or other shaped piece, the first peg in the row is skipped. Simply don't wrap or knit the first peg. It is referred to as skip 1.

SHORT ROWS AND WRAPPING THE PEG

Short rows are formed by only working across some of the pegs (stitches) before stopping and working back. This method adds extra length to some of the stitches for shaping such as on the Socks, Slippers, Flower and the Corkscrew Scarf.

When working short rows, it is necessary to wrap the yarn around an unworked peg before changing directions in order to prevent holes.

Work across the pegs indicated in the pattern. Wrap the next peg as follows:

Step 1: If you are working the e-wrap knit stitch method, bring the working yarn to the outside of the wheel **before** the next peg. Using the tool, lift the loop from the peg to be wrapped and hold it on the tool *(Fig. 17a)*.

Fig. 17a

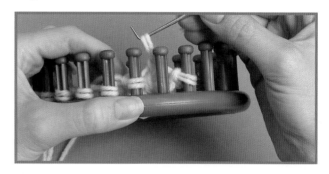

Step 2: Bring the working yarn behind the empty peg, then around the peg to the outside of the wheel *(Fig. 17b)*.

Fig. 17b

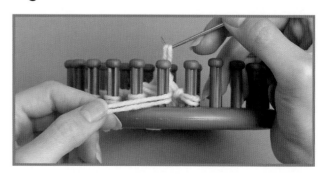

Step 3: Put the loop that is on the tool back onto the peg. The wrap will be under the loop *(Fig. 17c)*. Leave the remaining pegs unworked. If you are working the e-wrap knit stitch method, bring the working yarn back to the inside of the wheel so that it is in position to knit back in the other direction; leave the remaining peg(s) unworked.

Fig. 17c

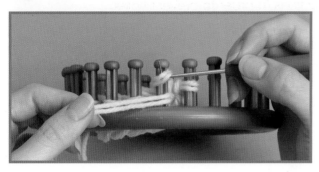

You will be instructed in the pattern when to knit the wrapped peg. To do so, e-wrap the wrapped peg and lift all the loops over the top loop and off the peg.

MAKING A CUFF OR VISOR

Begin project as specified in instructions. To form a Cuff or Visor, lift up the bottom edge toward the inside of the wheel and place the loops from the cast on row over the pegs *(Fig. 18)*. There will be 2 loops on each peg.
Work as instructed, securing the bottom edge and leaving one loop on each peg. This method can also be used to join ends together, as on the Flower.

Fig. 18

CHANGING COLORS IN INTARSIA KNITTING

Intarsia knitting is a technique used to knit isolated blocks of color without carrying the unused yarn across the back of the piece. A separate ball is used for each block of color. Where the colors meet, the strands of yarn need to be twisted in order to prevent gaps between the colors.

When changing colors, **twist the yarns** as follows: Drop the color that you are working with (old color) over the top of the color you will use next (new color) *(Fig. 19a)*. Then pick up the new color, trapping the old color behind the first stitch worked *(Fig. 19b)*.

Fig. 19a

Fig. 19b

Tip   Tangling occurs when working with multiple colors of yarn. Keeping the skeins of each color in separate containers, like freezer bags, will help in the detangling process.

GATHERED METHOD TO REMOVE PROJECT FROM WHEEL

This method is used to take circularly knitted projects off the wheel when it has a closed top (or bottom) such as hats and slippers.

Cut the working yarn leaving an 18" (45.5 cm) end. Thread a yarn needle with the end. Beginning with the last peg, insert the yarn needle in the next loop and lift it off the peg. Repeat for each loop around the wheel **(Fig. 20a)**.
With yarn end to the wrong side of the project, pull the end tightly, gathering the loops to the center **(Fig. 20b)**; knot yarn tightly and weave in the end; clip end close to work.

Fig. 20a

Fig. 20b

BINDING OFF

Binding off is a process that removes the loops from the pegs of the wheel and secures the stitches.

CHAIN ONE BIND OFF

Insert the crochet hook in the loop on the last peg and lift it off the peg. Working to your left, insert the hook in the loop on the next peg, lift it off the peg and pull it through the loop on the hook **(Fig. 21a)**, ★ chain 1 **(Fig. 29, page 55)**, insert the hook in the loop on the next peg, lift it off the peg **(Fig. 21b)** and pull it through the loop on the hook; repeat from ★ until all of the loops have been removed from the wheel and there is one loop left on the crochet hook. Cut the yarn and pull end through the final loop **(Fig. 21c)**; secure yarn.

Fig. 21a

Fig. 21b

Fig. 21c

RIBBING BIND OFF

The ribbing bind off method produces a nice finish to knitted garments that need some stretch like socks and mitts.

When ready to bind off, wrap the working yarn around the entire wheel 3 times and cut the yarn at that point, giving you a long enough length to sew with. Thread the yarn needle with the end.

Step 1: Bring the yarn needle down through the loop on the first peg to the right of where the working yarn is attached *(Fig. 22a)*.

Fig. 22a

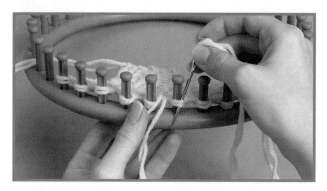

Step 2: Bring the yarn needle up through the loop on the peg to the left of this one *(Fig. 22b)*.

Fig. 22b

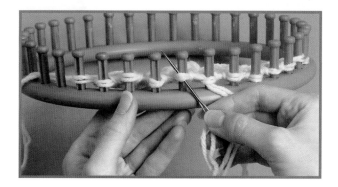

Step 3: Skip the peg to the right of this one (and holding the yarn behind the skipped peg, keeping it out of the way) insert the yarn needle down through the loop on the next peg *(Fig. 22c)*.

Fig. 22c

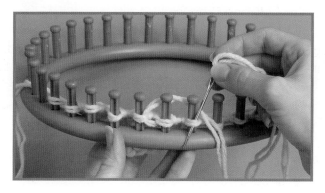

Step 4: Bring the yarn needle up through the loop on the peg to the left of this one *(Fig. 22d)*.

Fig. 22d

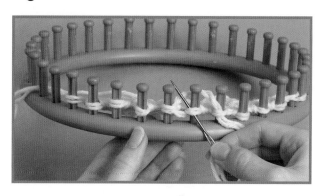

Repeat Steps 3 and 4 until all of the loops have been worked on the pegs. Remove loops from pegs.

> *Tip* While working this bind off, pull gently on the yarn end to keep the bind off loops firm. If the loops are too loose after removing the item from the wheel, adjust the bind off loops gently and take up the slack with the working yarn.

DOUBLE KNITTING

Double knitting is worked on the straight wheel. When working two pairs of pegs together, the knitting is a double thickness and is the same on both sides.

When instructed to **anchor yarn**, attach the end of the yarn to the side peg with a slip knot **(Figs. 27a-c, page 55)**. This holds the beginning yarn and also the working yarn until you are ready to use it.

> *Tip*   If you are holding two or more strands of yarn together, be sure to treat them as one.

DOUBLE CAST ON

The number of stitches you will be instructed to cast on are sets of pegs (one peg from the back and one peg directly in front of it).

Step 1: Holding the straight wheel horizontally in front of you and leaving a 6" (15 cm) end, insert the yarn end in the center of the straight wheel from the top to the bottom and anchor the yarn on the outside peg on the right hand side **(Fig. 23a)**. Once the anchored yarn is removed, the yarn end will hang to the inside of the wheel.

Fig. 23a

Step 2 (Foundation row)**:** Wrap the yarn around the first peg on the top row in a clockwise direction **(Fig. 23b)** and around the bottom peg in a counter-clockwise direction **(Fig. 23c)**, forming a figure eight. Continue across, wrapping the yarn around the next peg on the top row in a clockwise direction and around the bottom peg in a counter-clockwise direction until all of the pegs needed have been wrapped, pushing the loops down as you go.

Fig. 23b   **Fig. 23c**

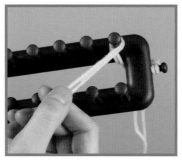 

> *Tip*   The yarn should cross at each peg at the inside of the wheel **(Fig. 23d)**, leaving a loop on the outside of each peg.

Fig. 23d

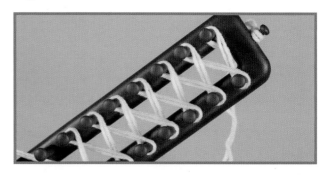

DOUBLE KNIT STITCH

Step 1: Skip the last peg wrapped, as it will not be wrapped a second time. Move yarn straight up and wrap the yarn around the first peg on the top row counter-clockwise **(Fig. 24a)**. Wrap the second peg on the bottom row clockwise **(Fig. 24b)**. Following the path of the yarn on the foundation row, continue across, wrapping the yarn around the next peg on the top row in a counter-clockwise direction and around the bottom peg in a clockwise direction until all of the pegs have been wrapped, pushing the loops down as you go. There will be one loop on the skipped peg and 2 loops on all the other pegs.

Fig. 24a

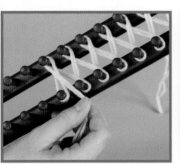

Fig. 24b

Note: If the yarn has been wrapped too tightly, it will be very difficult to lift the bottom loop over the top loop (Step 2). If this is a problem, remove the yarn and rewrap again, working looser.

Step 2: Using the tool, lift the bottom loop on the last peg wrapped over the top loop and off the peg **(Fig. 24c)**. This completes the stitch and secures the working yarn. Continue across both sides of the straight wheel. Your first row of knitting is complete **(Fig. 24d)**.

Fig. 24c

Fig. 24d

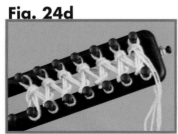

Note: The stitches will be loose and the work will come down through the center slot of the wheel as work progresses.

Step 3 (Wrapping row): Skip the last peg wrapped, as it will not be wrapped a second time. Working across the straight wheel from right to left, wrap the yarn around the first peg on the bottom row counter-clockwise. Wrap the second peg on the top row clockwise **(Fig. 24e)**. Following the path of the yarn on the previous row, continue across, wrapping the yarn around the next peg on the bottom row in a counter-clockwise direction and around the top peg in a clockwise direction until all of the pegs have been wrapped, pushing the loops down as you go. There will be one loop on the first peg and 2 loops on all the other pegs.

Fig. 24e

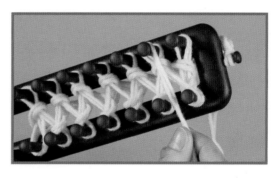

Step 4 (Completing stitches): Using the tool and beginning with the last peg wrapped, lift the bottom loop on each peg over the top loop and off the peg.

To form remaining rows, skip the last peg wrapped and continue wrapping following the figure 8 pattern established. There will be one loop on the first peg of each wrap sequence and 2 loops on all the other pegs. Repeat Step 4 to complete the stitches **(Fig. 24f)**.

Fig. 24f

Note: After working 3 or 4 rows, remove the anchored yarn from the side peg and allow the bottom of the piece to hang free.

Chain 1 Bind off: Using a crochet hook, insert the hook in the loop on the first peg and lift it off the peg, insert the hook in the peg straight across, lift it off the peg and pull it through the loop on the hook **(Fig. 25a)**, ★ chain 1 **(Fig. 29, page 55)**, insert the hook in the loop on the next peg diagonally across, lift it off the peg and pull it through the loop on the hook, chain 1, insert the hook in the loop on the next peg straight across, lift it off the peg and pull it through the loop on the hook; repeat from ★ until all of the loops have been removed from the wheel and there is one loop on the crochet hook. Cut yarn and pull the end through the final loop **(Fig. 25b)**; secure yarn.

Fig. 25a

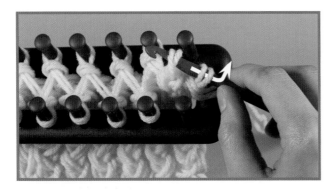

Fig. 25b

I-CORD

I-cord is a narrow tube of knitting that can be used as ties for a wrapped sweater or can be attached to ear flaps on a hat.

★ Do **not** knit back the other direction. Instead, bring the working yarn from the last peg worked, along the back of the pegs, to the first peg that was worked **(Fig. 26a)**. E-wrap and knit the pegs in the same direction as the previous row **(Fig. 26b)**; repeat from ★ until length indicated in instructions is obtained.

Fig. 26a

Fig. 26b

FELTING

Felting happens when you do what mother told you not to do to your wool sweaters—wash them in hot water! Wool will shrink and the stitches meld together to become a solid piece of felted cloth when agitated in hot water.

The felting projects in this leaflet use yarns with at least 80% wool content. Using a yarn with higher wool content will make the felting process more successful. If wool yarn is super washed, it will **not** felt.

To felt your knitted project, place it in a zippered pillowcase or lingerie bag. Toss it into your washer with a pair of jeans and a small amount of detergent. Wash project in hot water on the regular cycle to agitate. Set a timer for 3 to 5 minutes so that you can check the felting progress. Please remember this is hot water! Use caution when checking the project so that you do not scald your hands. When you stretch the knitting and are unable to see the defined stitches, the project is felted. Continue setting timer for 3 minute intervals and checking the felting progress until it is completed. **Watch it carefully! The longer the project is in the washer, the more it shrinks!**

Once the project is felted, remove it from the washer, hand rinse in warm water, and pat dry with a towel. Do **not** put your project in the dryer, as it will continue to shrink and change it's shape. Shape the project (over an item the same shape and size of your piece) and allow to air dry. It may take several days.

Basic Crochet Stitches

SLIP KNOT

Make a circle and place the working yarn under the circle **(Fig. 27a)**. Insert the hook under the bar just made **(Fig. 27b)** and pull on both ends of the yarn to complete the slip knot **(Fig. 27c)**.

Fig. 27a   **Fig. 27b**   **Fig. 27c**

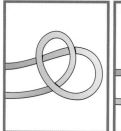  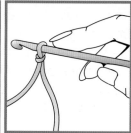

YARN OVER

Bring the yarn over the top of the hook from back to front, catching the yarn with the hook and turning the hook slightly toward you to keep the yarn from slipping off **(Fig. 28)**.

Fig. 28

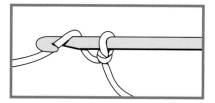

CHAIN

Yarn over **(Fig. 28)**, draw the yarn through the loop on the hook **(Fig. 29)**.

Fig. 29

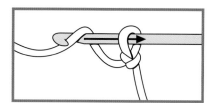

Yarn Information

The items in this leaflet were made using a variety of yarns. Any brand of the specified weight of yarn may be used. It is best to refer to the yardage/meters when determining how many balls or skeins to purchase. Remember, to achieve the same look, it is the weight of the yarn that is important, not the brand of yarn.

For your convenience, listed below are to specific yarns used to create our photo models.

FAUX FEATHER BOA
Patons® Bohemian
#11108 Beatnik Blues

BASKET HAT
Patons® Shetland Chunky Tweed
#67108 Medium Blue Tweeds

VISOR CAP
Red Heart® Classic®
#971 Camouflage

FUR STRIPES EAR FLAP HAT
Red Heart® Super Saver®
#318 Watercolor
Lion Brand® Fun Fur
#191 Violet

FINGERLESS MITTS
Lion Brand® Jiffy®
#145 Plum

BLANKET PONCHO
Lion Brand® Lion Suede
#205 Waterlilies Print

DOUBLE KNIT SCARF
Caron® Perfect Match®
#7416 Mixed Greens Ombre

IRISH LASS BERET
Caron® Perfect Match®
#7416 Mixed Greens Ombre

CORKSCREW SCARF
Patons® Allure
#04208 Turquoise

ADULT SOCKS
Patons® Classic Merino Wool
#77732 That's Pink

INFANT SOCKS
Bernat® Softee® Baby
#02003 Lemon

COZY QUILT
Lion Brand® Pound of Love
#157 Pastel Yellow
#101 Pastel Pink
#106 Pastel Blue

CHECKERED FLAG SCARF
Caron® Bliss
White - #0001 Snow
Black - #0013 Black

FELTED FEDORA
Patons® Classic Merino Wool
Main color - #00230 Bright Red
Contrasting color - #00212 Royal Purple

FELTED FLOWER
Patons® Classic Merino Wool
#00230 Bright Red
#00212 Royal Purple

FELTED WALLET BELT
Patons® SWS
#70117 Natural Denim

FELTED SLIPPERS
Patons® Classic Merino Wool
#00231 Chestnut Brown

IT'S A WRAP SWEATER
Patons® Shetland Chunky Tweeds
#67532 Deep Red Tweeds